PILGRIMAGE OF GRACE

Cardinal Basil Hume, 1923-1999

PILGRIMAGE OF GRACE
Cardinal Basil Hume, 1923-1999

Kevin Nichols

VERITAS

First published 2000 by
Veritas Publications
7/8 Lower Abbey Street
Dublin 1

ISBN 1 85390 389 2

Cover design by Colette Dower
Cover photograph courtesy of Archdiocese of Westminster
Printed in the Republic of Ireland by Betaprint Ltd, Dublin

A Collection of Epitaphs

Basil Hume died peacefully in London on a June evening in 1999. At the same time in his native North, a laggard summer was with difficulty shouldering its way through the remains of a bleak spring.

His death was not unexpected. Only a few days earlier he had received from the Queen the highly prestigious Order of Merit – his last public appearance – and the media were instantly loud with his praises. Within hours of his death BBC television altered its programmes to broadcast a documentary of his life. The following week the whole of his funeral was televised. Among the tributes from his friends, perhaps the most touching and the deepest-reaching came from the Chief Rabbi. Dr Sachs invoked the early sages of Israel who taught that a hero is 'one who turns strangers into friends … he knew that those whose faith is deepest reach the point where, transcending boundaries, soul speaks to soul. Out of that conversation, true peace is born'. Lord Runcie wrote of 'the shy monk who … grew in grace to become one of the great spiritual leaders of our time'. Others spoke of his personal qualities – a humility that was refreshing and arresting in the age of image and sound-byte, a loyalty and faithfulness held in equilibrium with open-mindedness and courage.

Others scrutinised his achievements as a public figure of wide influence. His style of leadership was, it seemed, very different from that of his predecessors; more subdued, more alert, more sensitive. His interventions in public affairs, sometimes open and dramatic, sometimes oblique and scarcely noticed, were most often effective. Above all, his ministry in his high office was judged to have a quality that was new in an elusive but substantial way, best described by words like 'tone' and 'timbre' and 'style'. He related to his own Church community in a way that was subtly but deeply different from the past, which many found affirming, reassuring and life-giving. He also spoke to and was heard by a larger constituency, by the national community as a whole. In doing this successfully he altered the position and character of his own Church as a component of national life. In the past it had stood on the margin of that life, viewed as alien and with some suspicion. Of course a process of assimilation had been going on long before he took office. He accelerated this, though he was well aware that it posed certain problems concerning the identity and the character of the Catholic Church in England.

These accolades for a Catholic Archbishop of Westminster were unprecedented. In 1850, *The Times* had given his earliest predecessor in that see, Nicholas Wiseman, a chilling reception: 'If this appointment be not intended as a clumsy joke, we confess that we can only regard it as one of the grossest acts of folly and impertinence which the court of Rome has ventured to commit since the crown and people of England threw off its yoke.' In 1999, *The Times* not only printed a generous obituary but also devoted four pages to an account of Cardinal Hume's life. No doubt Cardinal Wiseman, saturated in Romanità, had completely misjudged the situation in England and had failed to foresee the hostility and fear that his triumphalist entry provoked. Partly because of that, those who followed him in Westminster kept for the most part a low profile. Their world was the world of the Roman congregations and colleges, of the 'mother church' in Ireland, of diocese, seminary, monastery and convent, of rigorous obedience and personal piety. When it was necessary to become involved with the larger world outside, they would do so by way of a cautious *ostpolitik*; to negotiate if one had to but to do so with a fairly long spoon. They and their colleagues built up in the Catholic Church in England a strong minority morale, a desire for self-sufficiency and a strong sense of separateness, based indeed on a long and heroic tradition.

Even Basil Hume's immediate predecessor, Cardinal John Heenan, shared this rather wary and defensive outlook on the larger society. Although a gifted and generous-hearted man and a notably successful performer on radio and television, he seemed uneasy in the world of political realities, social change and academia. One aspect of the differentness of Basil Hume's archbishopric was that he seemed able to enter into those worlds with ease and without anxiety, though he did, in his disarming way, introduce himself to an audience of distinguished barristers as feeling 'like an alley cat who has strayed by accident into Crufts'. His ability to do these things stemmed from his origin and upbringing, from the deeper reaches of his life and from that bright line of grace and destiny that, as we see now, sustained his life.

In My Beginning is My End

Ellison Place is embedded now in the academic sprawl of the University of Northumbria in Newcastle-upon-Tyne. Only half a terrace remains of handsome if rather heavy Victorian houses containing, amongst other things, the main University offices. Many years later, the Cardinal was to remark on the strange patterns that surface in the whirligig of human affairs, when he received an honorary doctorate in law from the University. It was here that Basil Hume was born in 1923 and grew up with his three sisters and his brother. His father, Sir George Hume, a Scots Presbyterian, was a physician specialising in heart-disease. His mother, formerly Marie Elizabeth Tissère, was the daughter of a French general. No doubt he drew something from all the strands in his varied heritage; an ecumenical concern, for one thing, and a certain Gallic reasonableness, a feeling for Europe, a little in the spirit of Hilaire Belloc. He grew up bi-lingual in French and English. He spoke with great warmth and affection of his parents and no doubt his happy home explains why he appeared (and fundamentally was) so secure a person, not thrown by change and circumstance, unafraid of launching out into the deep.

Ellison Place in those days was on the northern fringe of the city, close to the hospital where his father's work was. He grew up there in relative affluence and modest privilege. These facts of his early life – along with the fact that he was an Oxford man – account in part for the ease with which he was able to move among the great and the good and weave his way, unseduced but not unnoticed, through the corridors of power. It is a partial explanation. There were other and deeper reasons.

Behind the tranquilities and ample comfort of Ellison Place lay the rest of the city, the commerce and industry of Northumberland Street, Grainger Street and the Quayside, the 'teeming masses' who lived in poverty and wretchedness in Byker and Shieldfield and Scotswood. Times were hard. The 'land fit for heroes' promised during the First World War had proved a sad disappointment. Post-war debt, economic blundering and sheer lack of will had depressed the old industries – coal, steel, shipbuilding – on which the North East's daily bread depended. Unemployment was widespread, housing squalid, disease and premature death frequent. The general strike was imminent and Basil Hume was still a boy when the Jarrow marchers made their weary, dignified way to London, providing a stark, memorable image of the problems of the day.

There were plenty of people in the affluent suburbs for whom these wretched conditions were shrouded in a cloud of unknowing. Basil Hume was lucky (we can say with hindsight) in being brought face to face with them. At the edge of Shieldfield and Byker stood, and stands, a Dominican priory. One of the priests in that community, a friend of the Hume family, used to take the boy Basil with him when he visited his parish. Thus Basil came to see children without shoes, and families living in a single damp, comfortless room. He was able to sense the atmosphere of misery and hopelessness. He was morally sensitive enough to develop an indignation at the unfairness of it, an eagerness for justice and a compassion that never left him. He never lost his affection for his native city; his loyalty to the football team is well-known and much publicised. However, its greatest legacy was to keep him clear as monk and as archbishop of that 'fugitive and cloistered virtue', which John Milton said that he could never praise.

The only television programme that he made was about those saints, Aidan, Cuthbert and Bede, who in the seventh and eighth centuries had made Northumbria, for a brief while, a major and influential centre of Christian culture. He grew up in their shadow and found in their lives and writings a sense of history, a feeling of continuity and rootedness. His ecumenical work (so notably successful at least in his own life and relationships) drew much of its motivation and its character from the conviction of a shared inheritance.

Monastic Years

> God gave all men all earth to love
> But since man's heart is small,
> Ordained for each one place to prove
> Beloved over all
> — Hilaire Beloc, 'The South Country'

No doubt we can serve God and grow in holiness anywhere. No doubt tough Council estates, leafy suburbs and mountain fastnesses have each their grace of place. All the same, we are caught up in the 'scandal of particularity'. God became man at one particular historical moment, in one neighbourhood, within one culture and tradition, and his word was, humanly speaking, formed by those facts. We neither exist as nor are shaped by generalities. Rather, as Belloc observed, it is the particular we are attached to and the particular that forms our being.

Basil Hume went to the Benedictine Abbey School at Ampleforth in 1934. He remained there, as schoolboy, as monk, as abbot, for more than forty years. The buildings of the abbey and school at Ampleforth cluster in a broad, green, pastoral valley in North Yorkshire. Beyond it the ground rises and dissolves into the moors, which stretch, beautiful but sombre, to the North Sea. This was the place in which Basil Hume would act out his personal drama. It would deeply mark him, engage his heart, be the place that, as Gerard Manley Hopkins wrote of the Welsh Mountains, 'most sways my spirits to peace'.

The monastic family that Basil Hume joined was a Benedictine community of central tendency; it was not marked by the grim rigours of La Trappe, its bleak asceticism, its blind obedience. It drew rather on the humanity and gentleness that is so marked a characteristic of St Benedict's rule. The monk is to be a 'soldier of Christ' certainly, called to 'renounce his own will to fight for the King Christ ... taking up the strong and glorious weapons of obedience'. Yet, though the language is military, the spirit is not. The abbot is to act with prudent moderation. He must 'distrust his own frailty and remember that the bruised reed is not to be broken'. He must be balanced and take into account the realities of our human condition. So although perhaps ideally monks should not drink wine, nevertheless 'since the monks of our day cannot be convinced of this, let us at least agree to drink moderately, and not to the point of excess'. Monastic life is to go with the grain of nature rather than cutting against it. There is no talk of 'breaking the will'. Rather it is the common life that is the greatest mortification. What counts most in a monk's formation is the relationships he has with the abbot, with his fellow monks, with the visitors, with the sick. It is what he invests in these and the effect they have on him that shape his life and carry him forward.

The mix of fraternity and friction that constitutes community life is one of the factors that make the monastery into a 'school of the Lord's service'. But larger forces are also at work there. The very fabric of monastic life is prayer both as a common discipline and as a personal reality. The monastery is meant to sow 'seeds of contemplation'. Yet Benedictine tradition does not track the individual pilgrimage towards mysticism in the manner of St John of the Cross or the Cloud of Unknowing: 'Let us be sure that we shall not be heard for our much speaking but for the purity of heart and tears of compunction … our prayer ought to be short and pure unless it chance to be prolonged by the impulse and inspiration of divine grace'.

The central emphasis rather is on the 'Opus Dei', the work of God embodied in the liturgy of the Church. The round of offices and Mass shapes the monastic day. The larger cycle of season and solstice forms its year. The liturgy is a rich fabric woven from words, music and silence, from colour and symbol, from soothing repetition and salutary shocks. It moves through the year, re-enacting in its coat of many colours the mysteries of the Lord's life, re-creating the pattern of beginnings and endings, of death and resurrection, which is at the heart of his enlightening, healing, redemptive rhythms. Because of its richness, its many-sidedness, it is perhaps, among the several languages of faiths, the one that embodies in the most harmonious and life-giving way that transcendent mystery that is faith's object. It draws not primarily the mind through compelling ideas, not primarily the feelings through high drama, but the 'manalive', the whole person – mind, nerves, body, feeling, imagination. It offers, we might say, in modern terms, a formation of the sensibility. A formed spiritual sensibility is a huge strength. It enables one to meet the unfamiliar – the disconcerting changes that one encounters in life – without dogmatism, without aggression, without surrender, in a way that, by a kind of counterpoint, brings into being new insights and reconciling solutions. No doubt it was this quality in Basil Hume that the Chief Rabbi saw when he spoke of him as a 'man of God … who could speak about God in a secular age, and people listened'.

It seems odd to speak of a monk's 'career' as though he were an executive of the Midland Bank. All the same, monks train, do jobs, hold offices, move within the monastic ranks, sometimes upwards, sometimes downwards, sometimes sideways. Although Basil Hume studied history at Oxford and theology in Fribourg, he was never tempted to view academic life as an alternative vocation. He saw himself as a teacher rather than a scholar. He taught French to boys and theology to monks. The fact that he had to face the problems of teaching no doubt contributed something to the quality of the more complex, far-reaching tasks that lay ahead of him. Teaching is very different from academic study, though of course connected with it in important ways. The teacher must be concerned with the process of learning, with motivation and the attitudes of his students, with individual differences in ability and outlooks. Teaching cannot be kept in a cool, dry, germ-free place. It is inevitably plunged into the problematic variety of human life and human experience. It 'bears man's smudge and shares man's smell'.

This close attention to the complex realities of human life loomed even larger when, to no one's surprise, he was elected abbot of Ampleforth in 1963. The abbot, St Benedict said, must 'adapt himself to many dispositions. One he must humour, another rebuke, another persuade according to each one's disposition and understanding'. No doubt an abbey is more really and evidently a family than is a diocese, in which the priests are widely scattered and the bishop, inevitably an occasional visitor, can easily take on the appearance of a church official. All the same, St Benedict's advice has a wide relevance. A good abbot does not necessarily make a good bishop. Yet, those who have conscientiously and sensitively addressed themselves to the one task will have served a good apprenticeship to the other.

In this account of monastic life there are a number of *leitmotifs* – humanity, gentleness, prayerfulness, immersion in the deep rhythms of the Kingdom, realism, discernment, good judgement – which we can see are carried over into Basil Hume's life and work as archbishop. There is one other element that is not so obvious.

At first glance we might think that the life of a monk is very serene, stable and rather static. They live within an ancient and timeless order. Monasteries are usually planted in secluded places, safe from the world's contagion. Secular clergy are so-called because they live in the 'saeculum', in their own time, in the world. The use of the word implies that other priests do not. There is some truth in this and some falsity also. Ampleforth, with its prestigious school, has many connections with and very good information about the world, especially the large world of power and influence. But there is a deeper reason for doubting the image of monastic life as static and the monk as an otherworldly person.

Implicit in the idea of a 'school of the Lord's service' is the idea of movement, of development. In a school, if it is any good, the pupils progress, they do not stand still. Thus there is a dynamic element in monastic life as there is in any genuine spirituality. It is a pilgrim's progress. Significantly, Basil Hume chose as the title of his best-known book, 'To Be A Pilgrim', echoing John Bunyan's masterpiece. The word 'pilgrim' became a favourite of his, expressing a major theme of his life as monk and as pastor.

It is a word with a distinguished history comprehending not only Bunyan, but also the Second Vatican Council where the phrase 'pilgrim church' played a central and shaping role. It presented the Church not as a fixed and finished article, but rather as travelling through the currents and storms of history, looking for the ways in which it is called to change 'in order to remain the same'. It was an image that no doubt disturbed the even tenor of life at Ampleforth as it did throughout the Church. But it was one that Basil Hume took deeply to heart. There is, he said, no loyalty to the Pope that is not also a renewed commitment to the teachings of the Second Vatican Council.

A person who sees the Church in that way may well be a dynamic leader but is unlikely to be rigid. More than that, Basil Hume continued throughout his life to acknowledge that pilgrims will sometimes lose their way, that they will be dusty from the journey, that they will take some hard knocks and stray sometimes, like Bunyan's pilgrim, into Vanity Fair. 'A pilgrim wanders through life, often limping, sometimes bewildered, at times quite lost.' 'I go through life as a wounded pilgrim. It is very important to know one's woundedness and to accept it. I don't think I have ever met a person who was not in some way wounded, whether by their background, their upbringing, early disappointments, something that has happened to them or something they have done.' This acknowledgement of occasional bewilderment, lostness, vulnerability, proved in the long run to be one of his greatest strengths. People felt that he did not speak to them from a pinnacle but shared and understood their rather rickety lives. It was a rare and refreshing quality. Church leaders often present themselves or are presented by others as serene, complete and finished articles. This is not because they are not humble men but because they are overwhelmed by ecclesiastical propriety.

In March 1976, this particular pilgrim was, rather unexpectedly, appointed Archbishop of Westminster.

Transitions 1

An important issue in education has been, and is, that of transfer of training. How well will the knowledge, experience and skills that a person has learned transfer to a new and very different sphere of action? Will that person perhaps prove to have developed a tunnel vision, to be effective only among familiar landmarks? Will the brilliant goal-striker prove to be a poor manager of a club in the premiership? Or the excellent vicar-general make a poor fist of being a bishop? There are many people with skills that are so specific, experience that is so narrow, that they will only thrive in the setting within which they arose. On the other hand there is a kind of understanding that opens out onto wider horizons, a kind of experience that, learnt from, can be deployed in larger fields. Newman wrote of his ideal liberal education: it 'brings with it a power and a grace to every work and occupation which it undertakes and, enables us to be more useful and to a greater number' (J. H. Newman, *On the Scope and Nature of University Education* [Everyman, 1939], p. 160).

The archdiocese of Westminster and the Catholic community by and large were naturally a little apprehensive about these questions. A monk had never, in modern times, been archbishop, nor even a member of any religious order (though a few of each had held other sees). All had been drawn from among the secular clergy, usually after substantial experience in parishes, academic teaching in seminaries or experience in some form of church administration. Moreover, most had been educated at least partly in Rome and had acquired the elusive quality of Romanità. The word means far more than loyalty to the Pope. It implies having a nose for the way things go in Rome, a wet finger to detect the direction of the wind in the piazza outside the Holy Office.

The new archbishop was a bit of an unknown quantity at least as far as these categories were concerned. On the other hand, the times were uncertain, old formulas less secure. Perhaps someone from a very different background might do better. Monks, some reflected, had not stayed sequestered in their abbeys all the time. Frequently they had been missionaries – and the need for a fresh evangelisation was in the air. Often they had combined contemplation with active pastoral work, as Saint Cuthbert had done. In the Eastern churches bishops were almost always drawn from the monasteries. This practice served to underline the truth that a bishop's first concern is with the Kingdom of God rather than with efficient church administration. How would it go?

Transitions 2

The Archbishop of Westminster is not the primate of the Roman Catholic Church in England & Wales. Except as elected President of the Bishops' Conference he has no legal authority outside his own diocese. All the same, everyone knows that the Catholic community looks to him for leadership, and that the public world and the media are on the alert for his comments on critical issues of the day. So the new archbishop would be anxious to be aware of, and sensitive to, the character, the feel and tone and problems of the whole Church community. In the 1970s the archbishop would have needed particularly delicate antennae to achieve that awareness. Like himself, the Church community was making a transition.

After the Reformation, the practice of the Roman Catholic faith in this country became illegal. There was a burst of heroic martyrdom that established a tradition of courageous faithfulness. But times became easier, at least in practice, and the watchword was discretion and invisibility. The faith was maintained, just above freezing point, in a few dozen noble, recusant families and in some remote rural areas. Newman caught the spirit of the times in his sermon on the Second Spring: 'Here a set of poor Irishmen, coming and going at harvest time, or a colony of them lodged in a miserable quarter of the vast metropolis. There perhaps an elderly person seen walking in the streets, grave and solitary ... An old-fashioned house of gloomy appearance, closed in with high walls, with an iron gate and yews and the report attaching to it that 'Roman Catholics' lived there; but who they were or what they did or what was meant by calling them 'Roman Catholic' no-one could tell – though it had an unpleasant sound, and told of form and superstition.'

There were a number of strands in the Catholic revival that made a modest beginning about two hundred years ago. The Oxford converts established a small intellectual tradition, which included one thinker of huge importance for the future. They also introduced a devotional life that was ardent if a little flamboyant. Their numbers were few but the Irish immigrants who came seeking employment in the wake of the industrial revolution were very numerous. They brought their inheritance – a faith of great tenacity hardened by much suffering. The Catholic community grew, kept its collective head down, but built discreetly; especially it built schools.

Catholics were viewed with some suspicion. For the noble families, Catholicism might be shrugged off as a minor blemish. But for the rest, it was thought, their roots and deepest loyalties were not to queen and country, but lay elsewhere. They also lived for the most part in great poverty, indeed in ghettos. In the middle of the nineteenth century an early schools inspector wrote that only the Roman Catholic schools reach the very poorest children.

As a community, the Catholics tried to be self-sufficient; they built their own schools, trained their own teachers, centred their lives on the Church, kept themselves to themselves. They were highly disciplined. The Counter Reformation had effectively produced a Church that was strictly regulated, highly centralised, and very demanding in terms of doctrinal orthodoxy and moral rigour. No one took chances with the truth; Catholics proclaimed 'it is the Mass that matters', they were warmed by popular devotion and took a stern view of moral deviance. This thumbnail sketch is a little misleading, for in the rough and tumble of daily life, the Catholic community was a cheerful, good-humoured group, warm-hearted and closely bonded together. 'Do you kick with the left foot?' you might be asked. If you did, all doors would open for you.

In this small history, the Education Act of 1944 proved a major turning point. It provided the opportunity for students from the Catholic schools to find their way in large numbers to university. They came home again – most of them – having been immersed in the larger society and in strange intellectual disciplines. They formed a new presence in the life of the Church – not wholly alienated, but uneasy about some things and openly critical about others. They were of a piece with those working class students described by Richard Hoggart in *The Uses of Literacy*. Returning after university to their own culture, they were, he wrote, 'the uprooted and the anxious'.

As this movement got under way, the Second Vatican Council took place. At first it seemed to demand only some superficial changes, which were accepted, a little grudgingly perhaps but easily enough. In the late sixties, however, the deeper notes it struck began to vibrate – sometimes alarmingly – in the life of the Church community.

The ecumenical movement had already made a modest start. Now it gained full approval and gathered pace. The Catholic Church was no longer to hold its cards close to its chest. It was to pray with the other Churches. It was to look for common ground at all levels – in theology, in national life and locally in the parish. This was a new experience for Catholics, full of interest yet disconcerting also.

A deeper and more pervasive theme in the teaching of the Council was a certain shift in the relationship between the Church and the world, between religious life and secular realities. Catholics were to be less otherworldly, the Church less a self-contained system stretched above the facts of earthly experience. We were taught that 'the joy and hope, the grief and anguish of the men of our time ... are the joy and hope, the grief and anguish of the followers of Christ also'. Perhaps at first this sounded like a fervent appeal for wider charity. As it was developed, however, it turned into something of a Copernican revolution. We had always taken our agenda from above by a process of deduction. Now the realities of human experience – personal, social, economic, political – had also to be given serious attention. 'Taking one's agenda from the world', is a phrase that was sometimes used wildly. But it did fairly represent one aspect of the teaching of the Council.

These strong currents of change, following hard upon each other's heels, ruffled the smooth waters of Church life – at least to the level of a moderate chop. Because some of them were below the surface, because of the speed and power of mass communications, it was hard to assimilate and make sense of them. The sheer pace and the general air of shaking of the foundations were too much. Think of the year 1968. It was the year in which Humanæ Vitæ was promulgated, sending some shock waves through the Church and opening up some fissures. It was also the year when the Paris students took to the barricades; the year of the Tet offensive in Vietnam; the year of the assassination of Martin Luther King and Bobby Kennedy. Revolution all round seemed to be the watchword.

> Things fall apart, the centre cannot hold
> Mere anarchy is loosed upon the world.
> – W. B. Yeats

Inevitably members of the Church community reacted to these circumstances in various ways. Some, alarmed, withdrew into traditional certainties. Others took the plunge into newness with enthusiasm and sometimes rather wildly. It has been suggested that the Church divided into two the fortress church busily repairing the ramparts and raising the drawbridge against modernity, and the open church, influenced by and making common cause with the trends and problems of contemporary life. Yet those who see things in black and white are likely to fall victim to the disease of hardening of the categories. Things were not (are not) so simple but a good deal more patchy. A yearning for the past and an excitement about the future frequently co-existed in the same community, even in the same person. Perverse creatures that we are, we wanted to be ruled by the sharp smack of authoritative doctrine, and also to enjoy (as we saw it) the freedom of the children of God. The Catholic Church was not split in two; it was a little uneasy, beginning to decline in active membership, ready for a new and forceful leader.

Leadership

Cardinal Hume did provide that leadership in a rather unusual style. It was low-profile and self-deprecating. It avoided dragooning, hectoring or condemning. It was the reverse of the dramatic, eye-catching, sloganising manner in which most politicians construct their sound-bytes. It was not weak. On the contrary, Cardinal Hume took a firm stand on many issues; he had about him, one writer said, a 'steely mildness'. But it was a toughness without animus, a strength that shunned bullying. No doubt this reflected his natural character. Beyond that I think, it was his sense of the vivid presence of the love and grace of God that sucked out of his statements and decisions any trace of bitterness, personal dislike, contempt or anger. His Benedictine upbringing, as a monk and especially as an abbot, had given him a rare balance, a conviction that there are two sides to most questions, that few things should be brushed off as simply silly, that the weak and the misguided should not be mocked, that it is perilous to condemn others even in our hearts, lest, as St Benedict put it, we should forget our own frailty and break the bruised reed.

It is said that Abraham Lincoln remarked, at the height of the American Civil War, 'I have never had a policy. I have just tried to do each day, whatever God gave me to seem to be right'. Basil Hume would have felt a kinship with that statement. He did not have a policy the way political parties have them, though he did have clear priorities. There is always a tendency, indeed a perilous temptation, among Christians, perhaps especially among Church leaders, to transform faith into an ideology, to transmute that precious response to God's word ('Master to whom should we go?') into a complex, jointed, interlinked system of doctrinal concepts and moral principles. The virtue of an ideology is that its clarity makes it easy to develop a policy, to set up systems and institutions, to make plans, allocate resources and see what should be done. Of course, all religions need to go some way down this road. But to all these comes a dangerous critical point at which the ideology rather than the faith becomes the main factor in the Church's work and the source of its life. Dostoievski's Grand Inquisitor is a classic case of this transformation. It is a dilemma that is widespread in the life and history of the Church. It is not restricted to Catholic tradition. It is to be found also in Calvin.

Basil Hume did not go far down this road. He did not have much in the way of an ideology. He had a strong, deep and well-articulated faith. He had wide and generous human sympathies. He had a strong sense of the realities of grace at work in human affairs. While he always respected and lived within the doctrinal, legal and moral structures of the Church, it was from these personal qualities that the vision of his work sprang. He saw the Church at the service of the Kingdom of God. We can look at his work in three areas. First, there is the inner life of the Catholic community. Second, there is the mission of the Church to look beyond its own frontiers and to be, indeed, the servant of God's kingdom. Third, there is the Church at work in the secular city, striving to influence for the good its laws and institutions, and to give something to the quality of its common life. There are, of course, some issues that overlap these three fields of endeavour.

In the Household of the Faith

It is said that when Cardinal Hume came to Archbishop's House and sat down to his supper, he found the door leading to the house where the other priests lived, locked; and himself eating in solitary splendour. He sent for the key and joined them. This strikes me as being at least mythologically true. It is a parallel of the story of Pope John XXIII throwing open the windows of his office in the Vatican; a symbolic gesture of opening to the outside world, to the 'joys and hopes, the fears and anxieties of the people of our time'; 'We need some fresh air in here', it symbolically said. In a similarly oblique but unmistakable way, the Cardinal's open door spoke of a certain change of climate and attitude in the English Catholic community.

This appeared in its inner life and also in its external ventures ('the Kingdom'). The theologian Hans Kung was once asked why he, a noted radical theologian, focused so much of his attention on the life of the Church rather than the larger issues that preoccupy humanity. He answered, 'if things are not right in your own kitchen, how can you feed the world?' In the Catholic kitchen in the 1970s, there wasn't a drastic division into two; but there were some tensions, some cracks, some blocs that gathered themselves round a particular standard (traditionalist, radical, charismatic, evangelical, etc.). It is true that the Cardinal was archbishop of the Westminster diocese alone. Nationally his only authority lay in the limited powers that fell to him as President of the Bishops' Conference. All the same, the public eye – even the eye of the Church community – took little account of the canonical structures. The Cardinal was the one who had a national presence, the one to whom the media turned for comment on the issues of the moment, the one who was looked to for leadership in fact if not in law.

Naturally then, those who were partisans of a particular point of view were anxious to have him on their side. He was very careful about this. He listened with attention and sympathy to particular cases. But he knew that the Church's vision is usually larger than these and that his commitment of himself to them would tilt the Church in a partisan direction, thereby losing that balance, that universalising tendency that is an important mark of Catholicism. In 1996 he was persuaded to address a conference gathered under the aegis of Mother Angelica, the American TV evangelist. The agenda was to reaffirm the traditions and customs of nineteenth-century Catholicism and to condemn developmental ideas and modernising tendencies. He stood out determinedly against this, reminding the conference that there is no loyalty to the Pope that is not also a renewed commitment to the Second Vatican Council, that loyalty to the Church required loyalty to one's own bishop, that faith in search of understanding demands the right to explore and discuss, that the fellowship of the Church implies that we never damage another's good name but always affirm the good in others. It was a remarkable address, not a tactical gambit but one that sprang from his understanding of the nature of the Church, of authority, and the demands of charity and truth.

On this he had no qualms. But other issues arose, more specific, more complex, cutting nearer the knuckle. His stance against abortion was always resolute and clear. Yet some campaigners for the rights of the unborn child found his statements and actions on that question lacking in force. This was because he always insisted on treating abortion within its social, emotional, human context. Some thought that this blunted the keen edge of fighting for a pure and abstract principle. But he thought that in the tone and style of argument, abortion should not be lifted out of its social and emotional context as an urgent, agonising, human problem. The recognition of that, he believed, was demanded by both charity and justice.

As Cardinal Archbishop, Basil Hume was always scrupulously loyal to the Pope. He did not view the papal authority as a kind of last ditch defence of orthodoxy, an occasional exploding mine to warm us off dangerous roads. On the contrary he constantly defended the Pope's 'ordinary magisterium', that day-to-day teaching that is part of his office as universal pastor. Pope John Paul II recognised this in the letter written after Hume's death, calling him 'a shepherd of great spiritual and moral character, of sensitive and unflinching ecumenical commitment and firm leadership in helping people of all beliefs to face the challenges of the last part of this difficult century'.

Frequently decisions are made and messages sent by minor curial officials; and no doubt these are sometimes domineering and rude. When Basil Hume got one such letter quite late in his life, he thought that he, a senior cardinal, should confront the Roman congregation concerned. He did this (no doubt with his 'steely mildness') and observed, without malice but with the satisfaction of a job well done, the scarlet face that revealed the letter-writer. He was loyal but not servile. He believed in authority but not in despotism.

Some tensions, some conflicts even, do not invalidate fundamental loyalties. They may test them; strains and stresses are a necessary part of organised human affairs. They may also fortify them. The strength of these loyalties revealed itself during the papal visit to England and Wales in 1982. The visit began at a a tense time, its very existence threatened by the onset of the Falklands War. But these troubles quickly dissolved as its purpose and its character unfolded.

What is it that those who shared in it recall of that memorable event? First the huge crowds that attended the main rallies held in various parts of the country. No doubt we should not be too impressed with the fact of sheer numbers; still, they provided reassurance, injected fresh confidence and re-energised our common purpose. Second, the media reported both public events and private asides with considerable sympathy and warmth. A few centuries ago, an old woman is said to have greeted the news of the execution of Archbishop Cranmer with the words, 'The burning of the Archbishop hath burned the Pope out of the land, for ever and ever'. The visit marked a certain healing of these ancient conflicts, a forgiveness of ancient wrongs, the reconstruction at a popular level of a real, if limited, communion in faith and charity.

General principles, moral and doctrinal, are one thing. How they are put into practice in the concrete circumstances of our lives, in parishes, dioceses, countries, is rather different. Cardinal Hume knew as well as anyone else that some teachings to which the official Church is seriously committed (notably those on contraception) are not widely accepted in the Church community, not widely at all. He also knew that repetitious and rip-roaring condemnations would be not only ineffective but also discordant, contradicting other important principles in our faith. Conscience also has its claims. It is a difficult situation for any pastor. It is easy to give the impression of blurring, as Marxists might say, the party line; of falling into a kind of ecclesiastical *realpolitik*. After the famous 'Syllabus Errorium' of 1864, which condemned all things modern, Bishop Dupanloup suggested that official teaching represented a 'thesis' – what was ideally desirable in the abstract; practice depended on a 'hypothesis' – what should be done in the actual circumstances. Others have proposed the theory of gradualism – abstract moral principles represent an ideal not yet reached; we strive towards it, patient with the provisional.

I imagine that Basil Hume would have found the first of these theories over-academic. But the second one appealed to him. He saw that our time-conditioned lives are altogether entangled in gradualness, that this is obviously true of spiritual ideals but applies, *mutatis mutandis*, to moral principles also. Our grasp always exceeds our reach, 'else what is heaven for?' In the depths of his heart, in the depths of his faith also, he knew that principles cannot be applied to the realities of life, like a chemical formula to raw materials. He had a very good pastoral touch. He usually found the right words and gestures to reassure and encourage. He was able to lay an effective finger on the dense texture of fleshly reality. He knew – not as a theological conclusion but as a fact of experience – the truth of Karl Rahner's saying, that it is not that there are no moral absolutes, it is rather that in this bodily life, they do not occur in an absolute form. Both the principle and the concrete facts must be attended to.

'Sensitive and unflinching ecumenical commitment' was attributed to him by Pope John Paul II. His real friendships, personal and spiritual, with, for instance, the Archbishop of Canterbury and the Chief Rabbi, should not be dismissed as decorative. Personal relationships are always significant and, at that level, symptomatic of deeper changes also. It is true that the journey towards theological and institutional unity had reached an impasse. For instance, the Anglican-Roman Catholic International Commission was beginning to show signs of weariness and discouragement. But the Cardinal was not easily put off. He was instrumental in bringing the Pope and the Archbishop of Canterbury to pray together in Canterbury in 1982. In 1995 the Queen attended Vespers at Westminster Cathedral. He believed that that kind of unity would be fruitful and would draw other things with it. Perhaps this belief sums up all the aspects of his leadership within the Church. He 'was experienced by ordinary people as a call to prayer'. He saw all these matters as touched by the love of God. In that large embrace, our tangled lives, the dilemmas of the Church, the enigmas of the modern world appear in a different light, are conformed to a different order.

For the Kingdom

The distinction between 'maintenance' and 'mission' in the life of the Church is, though blurred, a useful one. Clarion-calls have often gone out urging the Church to lessen its introspective concerns with its inner affairs and look outwards to 'teaching all nations'. One aspect of this mission is a numerical one: to gather unbelievers into the visible frontiers of the Church; to re-activate the lapsed; to mobilise resources for the task of evangelisation. In Cardinal Hume's time at Westminster a number of very prominent converts were received into full communion and the fact was widely publicised. This gave to the image of the Church a certain buoyancy and drive, a sense of expansion and growing – an impression that a little reflection shows to be illusory. The number of active Catholics was dropping steadily, the number of priests decreasing drastically. Against the numerical yardstick, the 'mission' was not proving successful.

The mission, however, has another dimension. The Church can and often does reach out beyond its own frontiers not primarily with the aim of bringing in converts. Its purpose rather is to discover and work with the values of God, which are distributed piecemeal in the texture and fabric of human life. These values – justice, compassion, truthfulness, peacemaking – reflecting the Beatitudes of Jesus, testify the presence of God in the human world. Their absence or their opposite witness his denial. The service of these is the service of the Kingdom, to which, by its nature, the Church is committed. The Cardinal notably alerted the Church to this service and, by his personal influence, notably promoted it.

Baroness Shirley Williams has described how, arriving home late one night, she had difficulty fitting her key into the lock. Out of the corner of her eye she noticed two men on the street close by. She saw, to her surprise, that one of them was Cardinal Hume. His secretary came to help with the key, remarking, 'the Cardinal likes to see that everyone else is alright before he goes to bed'. It was a true and heartfelt concern. Everyone I meet, he said, has some personal sorrow to bear. Some he met had sorrows of a specially dramatic, indeed tragic, kind. His heart was drawn compellingly towards the homeless, the derelict, those who slept rough. He never patronised, but related normally and cheerfully to them. 'Do you know', one truly down and out greeted him, 'that I am wearing your trousers?'

These two small, haunting stories instance the truth that the Cardinal's concerns for the poor were an extension of himself. That they were very personal by no means implies that they were eccentric or amateurish, or that they were likely to crumble in his absence. He quickly perceived that the problems, troubles and pain on his doorstep in Westminster were serious, indeed scandalous. He set out to build a network of care, mobilising the resources of the diocese to provide what it could, and prodding other voluntary bodies, the government, the local authorities into action. This network includes a hostel for young people, a night shelter, a medical service and 'The Passage', a day centre for alcoholics and others, which offers refuge and also support and counselling. These form a net to catch those who are in immediate danger; they are linked to a number of half-way houses and more permanent homes. It is an impressive achievement, which has drawn support from the Department of the Environment and other public bodies. Ever anxious to avoid the impersonal, the neutral and the clinical, the Cardinal kept in close touch with these centres of care as far as he could. He related with unusual ease to those at the bottom of the social heap.

These initiatives embodied the gospel-value of compassion. Other events and persons brought him face to face in a vivid and challenging way with another beatitude, that of those who hunger and thirst for justice. In the late 1970s he was brought to visit a prisoner in Wormwood Scrubs. Giuseppe Conlon was a member of the 'Maguire Seven' found guilty of bomb-making in North London, who was also seriously ill. The Cardinal listened to his story and was left a little uneasy about the infallibility of the processes of justice. Subsequently he met Giuseppe's son Gerard who, along with the other members of the 'Guildford Four', was serving a life-sentence for a horrific bombing, which in 1975 had caused five deaths and many injuries. Although their appeal had been turned down in 1977, some voices – well-informed and responsible voices – continued to express disquiet over the justice of their condemnation. The Cardinal was impressed by this case and set investigations in train. He was greatly supported by the solicitors Alistair Logan and Gareth Peirce who generously gave of their time to work over the case and unearth its weak spots. Thus fortified, the Cardinal brought the matter before successive Home Secretaries. In the course of a visit to Mrs Thatcher, then Prime Minister, he spoke of the possibility that these men were unjustly imprisoned; Mrs Thatcher was horrified by this suggestion.

In 1986, Robert Kee, in his book *Trial and Error,* re-examined the case, querying the strength of some of the scientific evidence and alleging that some of the confessions on which the prosecution relied were forced. The tempo of public questioning quickened. Cardinal Hume led a delegation to the Home Secretary, Douglas

Hurd – a powerful and prestigious group that included two former Home Secretaries and two former Law Lords. Their submission, which included both a legal argument and newly uncovered evidence, finally led to the case of the Guildford Four being referred again to the Court of Appeal. This time the appeal was successful. In October 1989 the Guildford Four were released. Certainly the intervention of the 'Cardinal's Delegation' played a major part in this happy outcome. It also influenced, like a pebble pitched into a pool and causing ripples, the re-assessment of another similar case, that of the 'Birmingham Six'; they were also, in due course, freed. We have seen how in his early life a keen sense of fairness and an anger at injustice was awakened in the mind and heart of Basil Hume. Age did not weary it nor custom stale it. He wished, through his own person, to engage the Church in that quest for justice. Later he signed a submission to the Royal Commission on Criminal Justice, critical of the workings of the appeals system and of the fallibility of court procedures.

In the Secular City

It is often and rightly said that one of Basil Hume's most notable achievements was to make the Roman Catholic Church in England & Wales better-known, more widely accepted and more generally respected, its voice, therefore, more likely to be attended to. This put him in a strong position to make interventions in public affairs, to have some influence in social developments, to query the way in which bewildering technological progress is handled by government or viewed by public opinion. No doubt his own background helped him to relate with informality and ease to those who walk the corridors of power. But there was more to it than that. He saw human affairs both with an experienced and practical eye and also in the light of eternity. This gave to his perspective a certain depth and expansiveness, and a practical wisdom. Moreover he had taken deeply to heart the Second Vatican Council's teaching on the mission of the Church, especially on its responsibility within the secular city. The joys and hopes, the fears and anxieties that it finds there, it is to take to heart, in a way that is not partisan, in a ministry of service.

Some of the matters in which he intervened were issues with a strong moral charge to which the Church is directly and inescapably committed; as is the case with abortion law. But he had wide interests and concerned himself also with many questions that usually are not found in the centre of the Church's perspective. After the visit of Bishop Belo, he took up with the Foreign Secretary the matter of arms sales to Indonesia and in general. He joined with and supported the rising tide of protest at the manufacture and use of anti-personnel mines. He pleaded for more action to support refugees in Bosnia. He protested against the introduction of less generous treatment of asylum-seekers. At the end of his life he was trying to influence in some helpful way the intractable and worsening problem of Third World debt. Several of his interventions were concerned with international affairs. The moving photographs of the Cardinal at Auschwitz and with starving children at the height of the Ethiopian famine show that both the past and the present lay heavily on his heart. Not all of his ventures succeeded. Few of them were not carefully listened to.

In My End is My Beginning

In the spring of 1999, Basil Hume wrote to the priests of his diocese to tell them that he had terminal cancer. It was an announcement made in a calm, straightforward way without any drama or mystique. His illness progressed quickly. His reflections on the endtime are of a piece with his life. He had bad days that brought 'that common fear which tells us that there is no future, only a blank, nothing. We are no more.' He had even blacker days when he worried 'about the clumsy ways I have handled some people, about my selfishness'. Other mornings brought other thoughts. 'You have loved so many persons in your life; are you to be frustrated and denied what you have sought? ... It is not so.' There is an instinct towards survival in all living things. 'The mind says, ' It must be. It must be'. Then faith finally takes over and with triumph declares 'it is so'. 'The vision of God is that for which we were made. To see Him as He is, face to face is ... the ever present now of total happiness.' Though written in a special, in a 'limit' situation, these words ring true to our human experience of the ups and downs of faith, to the rhythms of our ramshackle lives. Yet they are transposed into the major key of joy and peace. Faith does not blank out our humanity. It does not abolish our failures or transform our humdrum sadness into permanent ecstasy. We are to persevere through our suburban squalor looking towards a lasting city. These are the words of a life-long pilgrim who never thought of himself as a completed article extracted from the human ruck, but whose faith was luminous enough to cast the light of God wherever he went.

That he died among fanfares of trumpets may seem a little surprising. For although he occupied a high office, his mode of occupying it was low-profile, was the reverse of flamboyant, was – to repeat a word often used to describe him – self-deprecating. Yet perhaps these are the very qualities that attract and impress us, denizens of the age of the cosmetic image. Perhaps also they conveyed effectively some sense of the geography of his inner self. His strength and flexibility sprang from an inner security, a natural wholeness irradiated by faith. His calmness, immunity from panic, refusal either to compromise or to bully, sprang from an inner balance that was both human and Benedictine. His openness of heart, his large compassion sprang simply from the love of God. Those who knew him, even from a distance, did not for the most part have clear or distinct ideas of these facts, still less articulate them. We often perceive truths in ways that are not intellectually systematic: as for instance in an icon, we perceive the mysteries of faith not through doctrinal formulas but rather 'in the deep heart's core'.

I end with a judgement that is more speculative, yet one that I make with confidence. It is that his life embodied in a luminous way the hardest and most elusive of all the Christian virtues – the virtue of humility.